Louis Harris – Carla Tyler

HOW TO PLAY

IN EASY WAY

A Complete beginner's Guide illustrated Step by Step.

Features, Easy Instructions, Practice Exercises

to Learn How to Play the Violin

TABLE OF CONTENTS

INTRODUCTION

This book aims to turn the real beginner into an authentic violinist. It's my dream to teach ordinary people how to really understand all the techniques and skills necessary for performing and mastering violin songs. I know how to break down the violin's complexity into small, easy-to-understand steps, so everyone can pick up a violin and play their favorite song. If you are keen on learning how to play violin skillfully, this book is for you!

You'll learn how to play melodies and studies in major and minor keys along with pizzicato, bowing techniques and a number of musical terms from this book. The examples contained in this book sound great and they're fun to play with. You will have a clear grasp of the basics of violin playing by the end of the book and even be eligible for more advanced study in Classical Music, Improvisation or both. It is recommended that you use a metronome with all the examples in the book to develop good timing habits right from the start until you can easily play them out of memory.

Using this book together with using sheet music to practice basic arrangements of a wide range of pieces by different composers is the best and fastest way to learn how to play a violin. This will help you create a repertoire and it means you have something to play with other musicians at all times. Practice and play as often as possible with other musicians. Learn by listening to the recordings you love. Start building an album collection featuring violinists you admire. Try to find sheet music versions, even if they are condensed, of the pieces you hear on the recordings. It will improve your pitch, timing and intonation by imitating great violinists.

This book unlike most other books is not just theoretical, it is practical and contains illustrative pictures to guide you through the entire process. It also concludes with practice exercises that will help you gain mastery of the violin.

However before you start playing, you first need to know and understand the parts of a violin as well as their use. Chapter one will help you get familiar with your violin.

CHAPTER ONE

GETTING TO KNOW YOUR VIOLIN

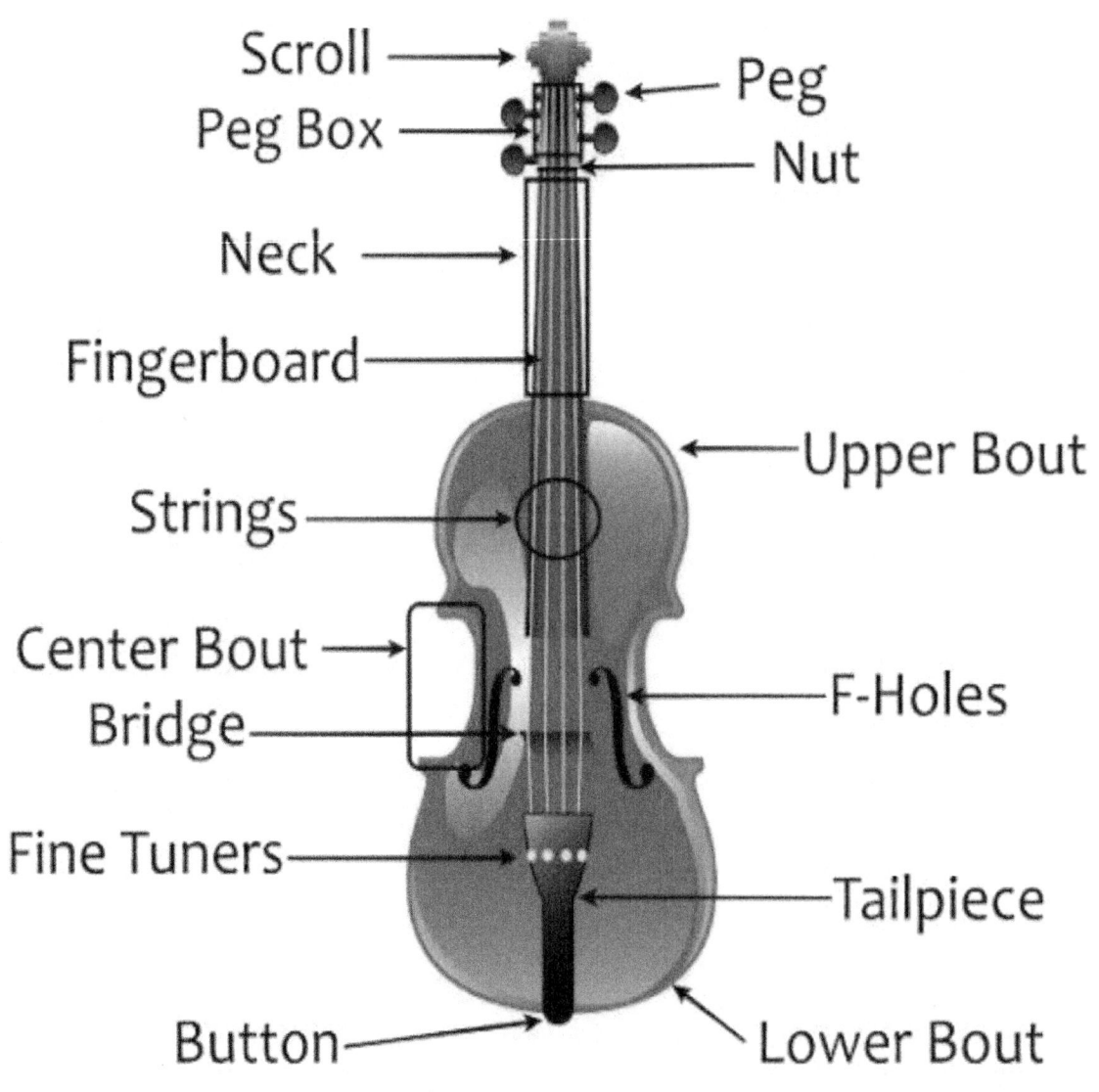

Scroll

Peg Box

Peg

Nut

Neck

Fingerboard

Upper Bout

Strings

Center Bout

Bridge

F-Holes

Fine Tuners

Tailpiece

Button

Lower Bout

The violin resembles the human body, with a front, a back, shoulders and a spine. The scroll is at the top of the instrument, a delicate carving that is like an old fashioned scrolled piece of paper. Below the scroll is the peg box which supports four pegs that are used in large increments to tune the four separate strings.

Just underneath the strings is a long black board called the fingerboard, which lets a violinist place pressure on the strings. The nut at the top of the fingerboard supports the four strings in air, and the bridge at the center of the instrument. The string ends are connected to the fine tuners, used in small increments to tune the four strings. The fine tuners are connected to the tailpiece, and a black-coated wire that coils around the bottom side button connects the tailpiece to the violin.

The F-holes are to the left and right of the bridge, allowing the sound to ring out from the violin. Learning the names of every part of your violin and bow is important. Do this every day for a few minutes until you get to know them from memory. Ask your instructor or a peer to test you on the names of each part of the violin.

THE BOW

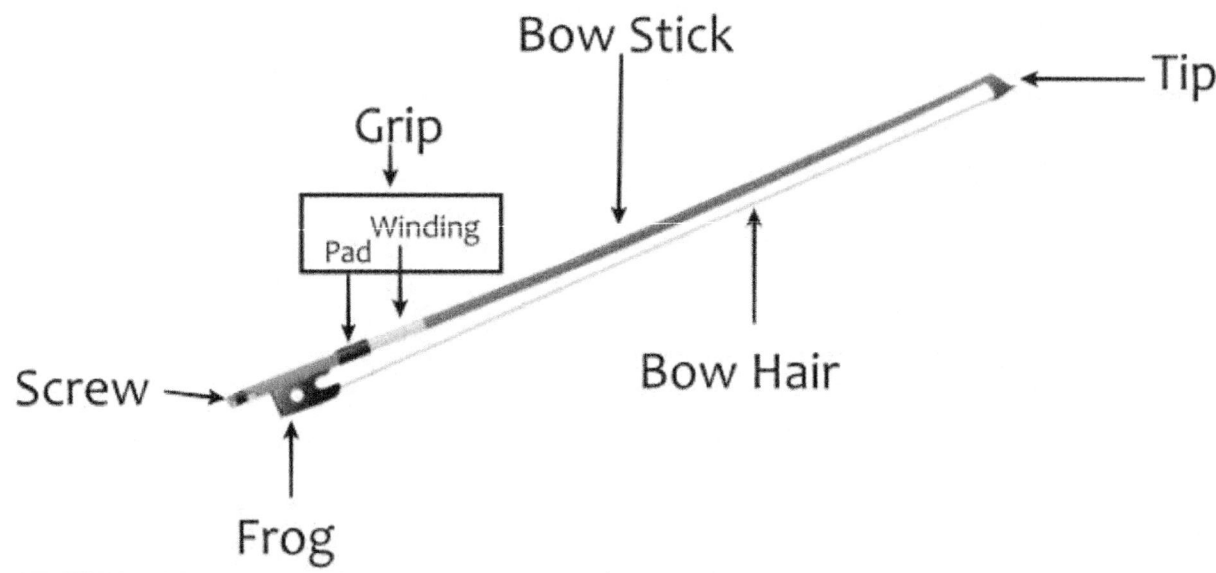

A bow consists of a specially shaped stick with other material that forms a ribbon extended between the ends of the string and produces sound.

Anatomy of the Violin

How would you go from tuning in to violin interpretations of your music the violin is made out of a body, neck, connect, melodic strings, soundpost, and a few different fittings? It likewise comprises of a tailgut, endpin, rear end, jawline rest, and tuning pegs.

The violin is somewhat curved at both the front and back and is thin at the inside. The body has adjusted closures that cause the instrument to seem like a little guitar.

Point by point Anatomy

All violins for novices have a similar fundamental anatomical part. Be that as it may, some are made of more excellent materials while others are worked for practice purposes alone. Here is a point by point take a gander at their life structures:

1. Body

Two curved plates make up the violin's body. They are connected to a rib laurel that incorporates linings, four corner obstructs, a top square, and a base square. The body frames an "hourglass" shape that is sunken on the two sides of the midriff.

2. Soundboard/Top

The soundboard houses the two sound openings. The gap is the place the sound departures from to make music. They arrive in an enlivening structure and are formed like a "f".

3. The Neck

The neck conveys the fingerboard, the parchment, and the pegbox. The last gives the basic mass to appropriately tune the instrument. It additionally gives the required grasp so the artist can hold the violin safely while utilizing one hand to tune it.

4. Scaffold

The scaffold seems like a spotted figure that has conspicuous medullary beams. It transmits the vibration of strings to the body of the violin. It additionally influences the sound that is being delivered by the instrument. The scaffold must be appropriately fixed and focused to abstain from distorting.

5. Sound Post and Brass Bar

The spirit or sound post helps bolster the top piece of the violin. It variably affects the tone created.

6. Pegs

The pegs permit the performer to change the tune of the violin. It has a silk folding over it to give rubbing. This piece of the violin must be kept up with peg drops to shield them from staying or slipping against one another.

7. The Bow

The bow is made of stick that has horsehair at the two finishes. It is a level material that is played over the strings to create music.

Selecting The Right Violin Size

Violins come in many different sizes, from the size of a toy to the full size of an adult, to fit any violinist's arm length. You want to measure the length of your arm from the middle of your left palm to the side of your neck when selecting a violin size, when your left arm and hand are fully extended perpendicular to your chest. The measuring system will perfectly translate into a correct fit, when extending the arm out. Sometimes your measurement may fall between the sizes of the violin, so it's best to choose the smaller violin until your arm and hand size can fully fit a larger violin..

STEP 1

MEASURE YOUR **ARM LENGTH**
FROM YOUR **NECK** TO THE
CENTER OF YOUR **PALM**

STEP 2

MATCH YOUR **ARM LENGTH**
AND **AGE** WITH THE CORRECT
VIOLIN SIZE

ARM LENGTH	AGE	VIOLIN SIZE
35-41	3-5	1/16
41-45	3-5	1/8
45-51	6-7	1/4
51-56	8-9	1/2
56-59	10-11	3/4
59+	12+	4/4

Selecting A Bow

A bow's shape is one personal choice. For greater control over minute musical expressions, I prefer a light, thin bow. For a louder volume a thicker bow gives more weight but tends to be stiff, making it difficult to control and achieve soft musical expressions. I also prefer an octagonal shaping of the round wooden verses on the wood. The octagonal shaping has a gradual increase and weight decrease throughout the entire length of the bow, which distributes evenly the vibrations traveling through the bow's wood.The bow and rosin work together to grip the string, creating a strong violin tone. Firstly, by turning the screw at the end of the bow clockwise to the right, you will stretch the bow to a pinky's width in the middle.

You will apply the rosin after the bow has been tightened by rubbing the sticky powder that forms on the bow's hair at the top of the rosin. A violinist is required only once or twice a week to rosin the bow hair. Always remember to loosen your bow hair before putting it back in it's case.

Useful Violin Accessories

These useful violin accessories are in the low end of cost and the high end of durability and reliability. This part will help you identify some of the best strings, shoulder rests, metronomes,tuners, and stands that will give you the most comfort, satisfaction and productivity.

Violin Strings

Take note of how the strings are labeled. The correct strings will make a big difference as to how your violin sounds. Choose a medium gauge on all four strings and a gold E string for bright and clear-sounding tones if you have the choice to choose the gauge and material of your strings.

The Shoulder Rest

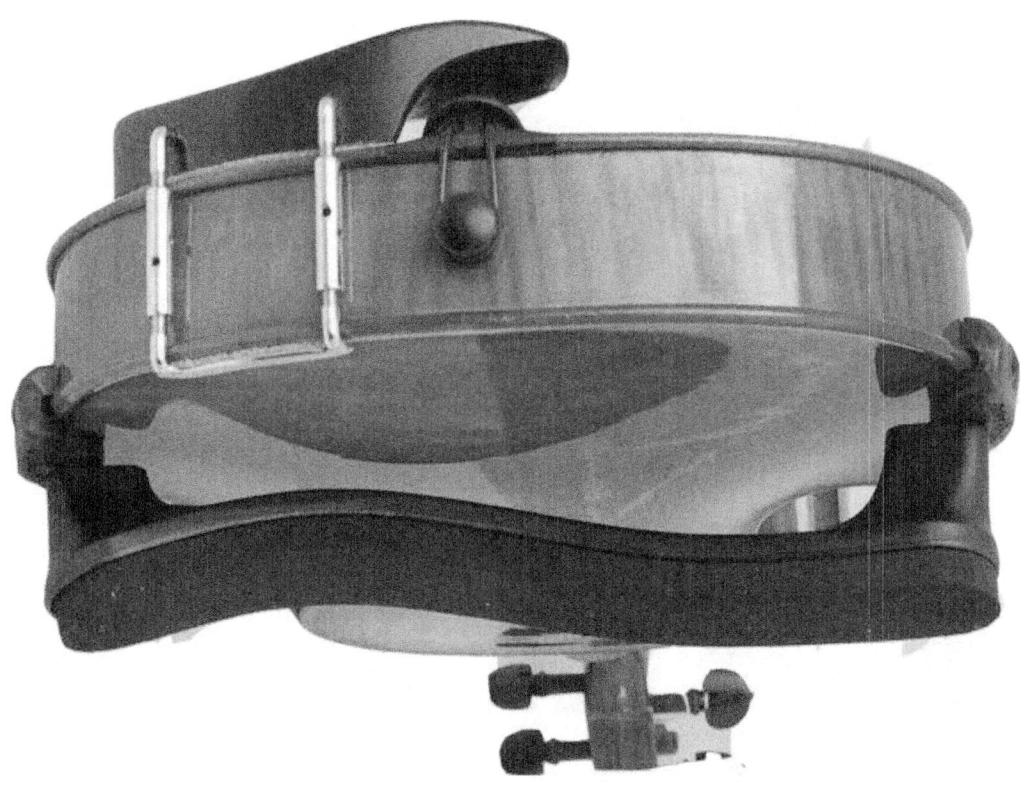

A shoulder rest can make it much easier to hold the violin by allowing the violinist to comfortably grip the violin between the underside of the chin and the top of the shoulder. A small child may prefer using a dry, natural sponge held by rubber bands on the violin, because the sponges are super flexible and easy to use.

Metronome

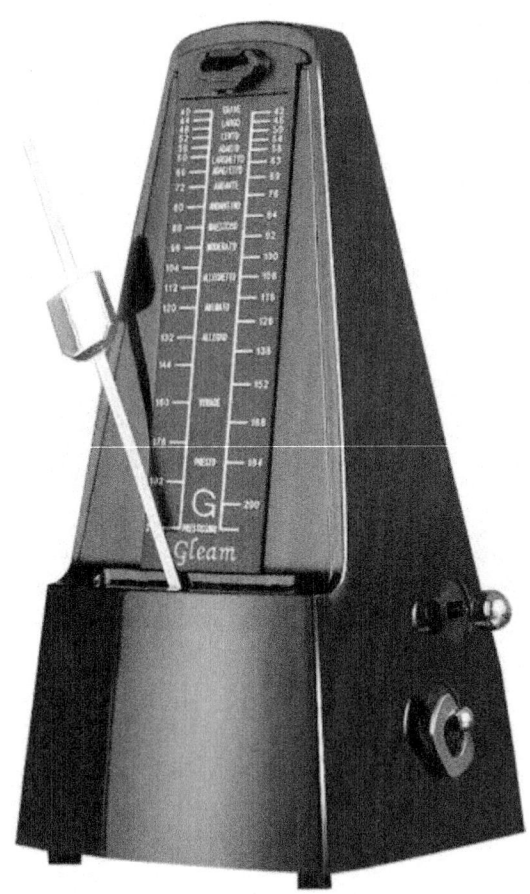

A metronome is a violin accessory that can make a student a true musician. A metronome at any tempo provides a steady counting rhythm that guides and reassures the musician for all rhythmic variations. Through changing the sliding weight attached to the pendulum shaft, the beat can be adjusted to any desired tempo.

The Tuner

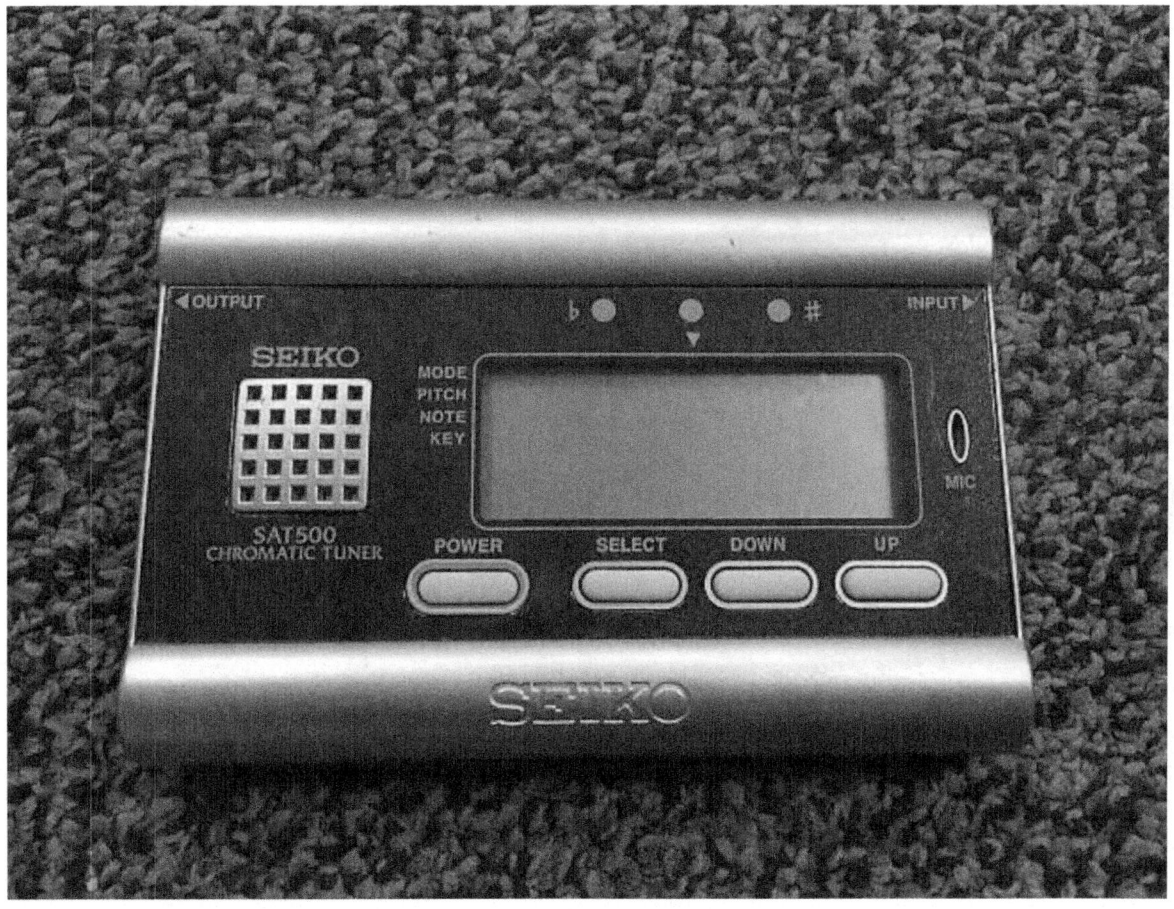

Every day, violin cords need to be tuned, and a good tuner is the best friend of a violinist. I found the most user-friendly to be the Seiko SAT500 Auto-Chromatic Tuner. Simply press the Power button, then play any string and it will automatically tell you what note you are playing and how far you are from the right pitch. No other buttons need to be pushed to tune different pitches.

The Metal Practice Mute

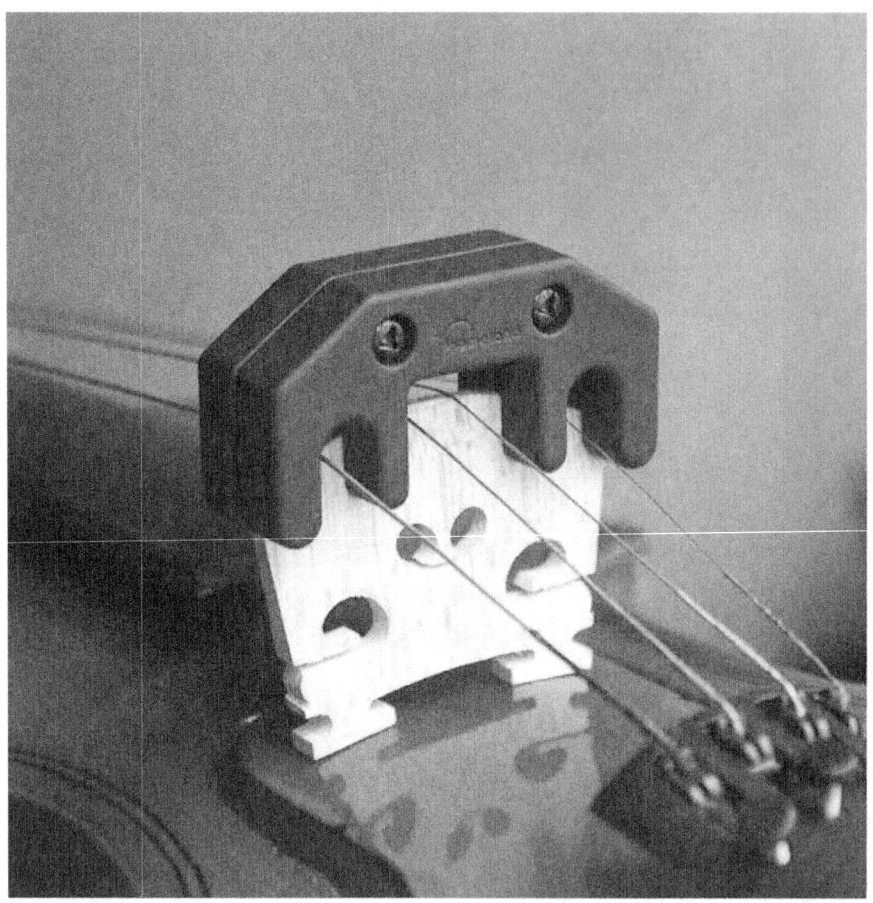

A metal practice mute is the ideal violin device for when you want to practice the violin without distracting anyone around you. The generic metal practice mute works by snuggly fitting on the top of the bridge and over the four strings; this minimizes the amount of vibrations from the string to the bridge, reducing the loudest of notes to a soft whisper significantly.

CHAPTER TWO

HOLDING/POSITIONING YOUR VIOLIN

Your body language, and the way your instrument is held, speaks volumes when it comes to your level of skill. Here's how to put the violin in the correct position of play:

1. **Rest Position**: This is when you place your violin on your right hip with your right hand holding the violin's lower side and your left hand holding the violin's lower shoulder.

2. **<u>Play Position</u>**: Grab the violin's shoulder with your left hand to stretch your left arm, and turn the violin upside down, counterclockwise, to take the instrument into play position. Place the right index finger on the down button.

3. **<u>Over Left Shoulder</u>**: Bring the violin over your left shoulder, until your right hand index finger hits the middle of your neck on the violin's bottom button.

4. **<u>Gently Securing Under Chin</u>**: Gently secure the violin in the chin rest with the underside of your chin, and gently raise your left shoulder. Lift your hands off the violin slowly and put your arms by your sides, holding the violin parallel to the floor with only your chin and neck.

5. **<u>Standing With The Violin</u>**: Be very careful that the violin is not dropped. At this stage you should be comfortably standing with the violin balanced between your chin's underside and your shoulder's level.

6.   **<u>Sitting Position</u>**: Turn the body to the right side of the music stand, so that the violin scroll is pointing towards the middle of the floor when seated. The feet should be divided, your left foot pointing toward the stand, putting your weight on both feet equally.

CHAPTER THREE

TUNING YOUR VIOLIN AND BOWING

When you have four fine tuners and the Seiko TSAT500 auto-chromatic tuner, tuning the violin is a simple process. Press the Power button on your tuner, and it should read 440 Hz automatically and in the C key without touching any other buttons. You must listen to the pitch of a violin string by pizzicato, or pluck the string, once you have the tuner ready.

Pizzicato

A good way to start playing the violin is to hold it in the playing position and play the open strings pizzicato, which means the strings are plucked with the bowing hand's index finger. Since you will not use the left hand to help play the notes, the strings will be represented as being open.

All beginners learn how to play the violin by pizzicato because to create a good sounding tone from the violin requires little background experience and little technique.

Here's the right way to pizzicato a note:

- Position the violin in play position and make a right hand fist.

- Use your thumb and index finger to make the letter "C"..

- Place the thumb at fingerboard corner.

- Set your hand side to the top of the wood of your violin.

- Slide your index finger like a finger trigger.

- Grab a string with your index finger pad and pull a medium-force string over it, making a pluck effect. You want to keep your index finger at about two inches from the end of the fingerboard when plucking any of the four strings.

Bowing

The first step in learning to use the bow is learning how to correctly align each finger with the required spacing on the bow's grip.

I prefer to use an ordinary, unsharpened pencil with a hexagonal shape, since a pencil has almost the same shape as a bow grip.

The pencil is lightweight, so you won't strain your fingers over, and at any time you can take a pencil to practice, which makes learning the bow hold on a pencil ideal.

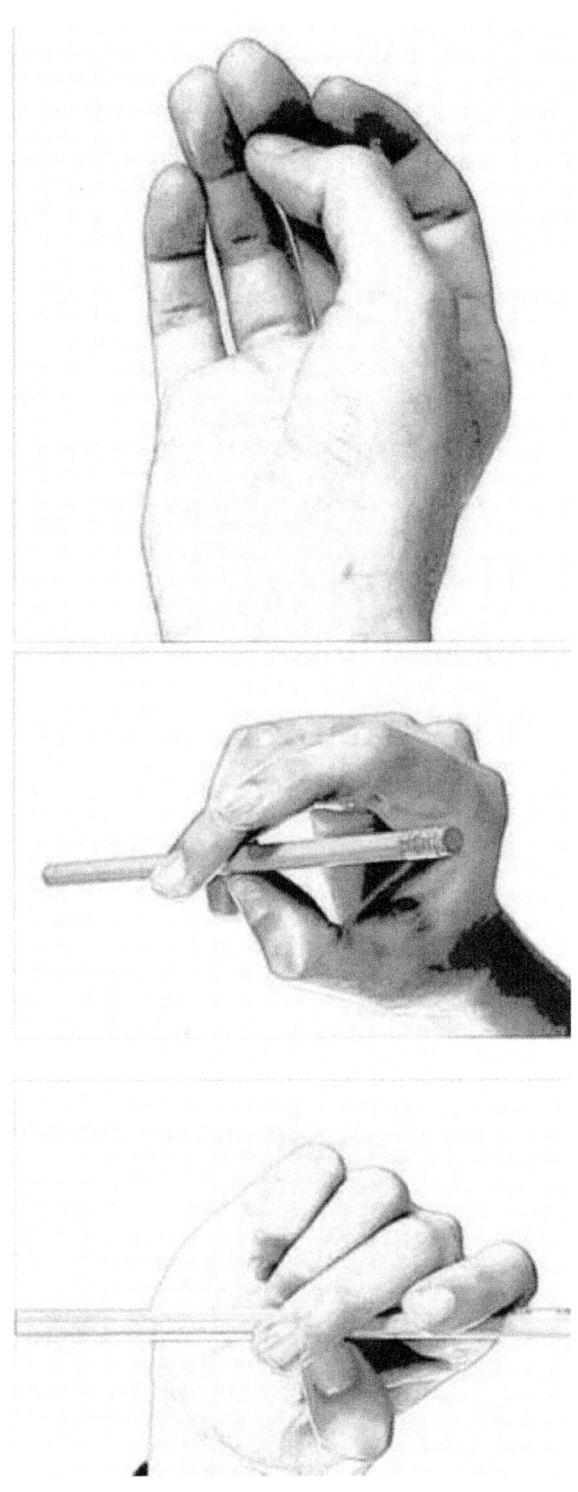

- Make your fingernails are all trimmed shortly. Place the tip of your thumbnail in the first crease from the end of your second finger with your right hand, and form a circle in the middle of the fingers attached.

- Insert the pencil center between the tip of your thumb and the crease of your second finger.

- Turn your hand to the left so that the pencil lies firmly between the first and second knuckles and touch the index finger pad along the pencil edge.

- Gently lower your third finger.

- Place a pinky, round on top of the pencil.

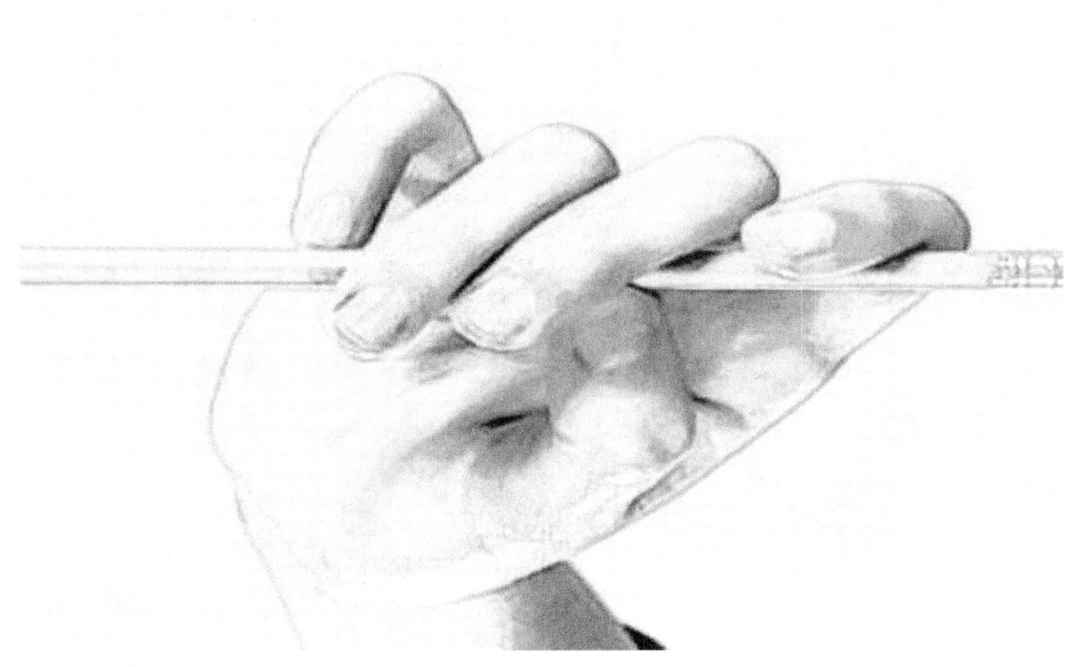

You'd eventually end up holding the bow like this:

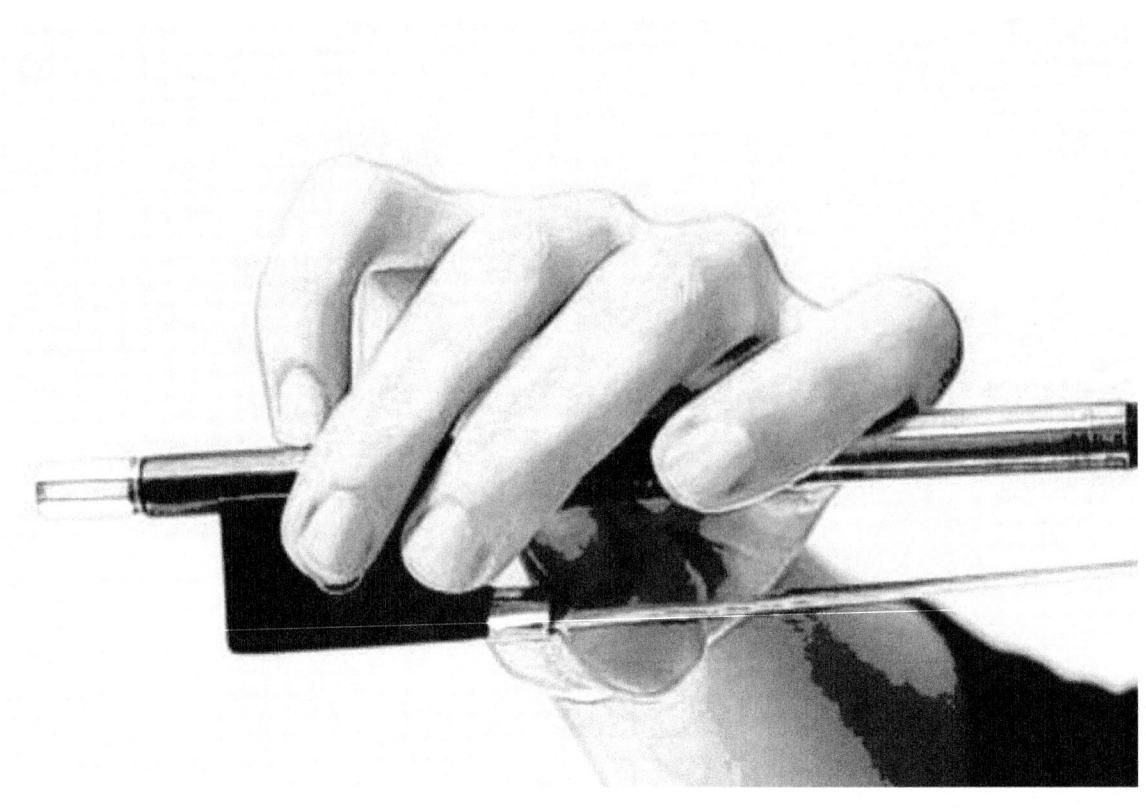

The bow should be kept parallel to the bridge and it should be at right angle to the violin strings.

CHAPTER FOUR

BEGINNING TO PLAY

The Finger Strike Technique

Memorization of the hand and the finger is critical when mastering the violin. The Finger Strike exercise will quickly enable your fingers to learn the exact spot for each note in each string by forcefully pinching your fingers at the center of each tape.

Easy way to learn the Technique of Finger Strike:

1.   Position your violin, your hand and fingers in play position, no bow.

2.   Strike your 1st finger down the A string violently, producing a thumping sound from the effect of your fingertip swiftly hitting the fingerboard string.

3.   Keep your finger at the exact location where the string reaches and see how close you are to the target tape center.

4.   Try again several times until you can perfectly strike your finger on the center of the desired tape.

5.   For each individual finger, apply steps 2–4, striking just one finger at a time..

The Cross Over and Hop Technique

One feature of a good fingering technique is the ability to hold down fingers when jumping and hopping on strings with other fingers.

This technique of holding down the fingers helps the violinist to use finger relativity for precise intonation to determine the right spacing.

Easy way to learn the Cross Over and Hop technique:

- Place violin, hand and fingers in playing position, no bow.

- Hold your 1st B round finger on the tip of your finger, on the A string.

- Set the 2nd finger to the A string for C using your red Low 2 tape.

- Hold your 1st finger B on the A string, while you "cross and hop" your Low 2 on the D string, A string, E string, and then return to the A string.

- Repeat this exercise while holding your first finger on each string as you turn over and hop your Low 2, 3rd and 4th fingers onto the surrounding strings.

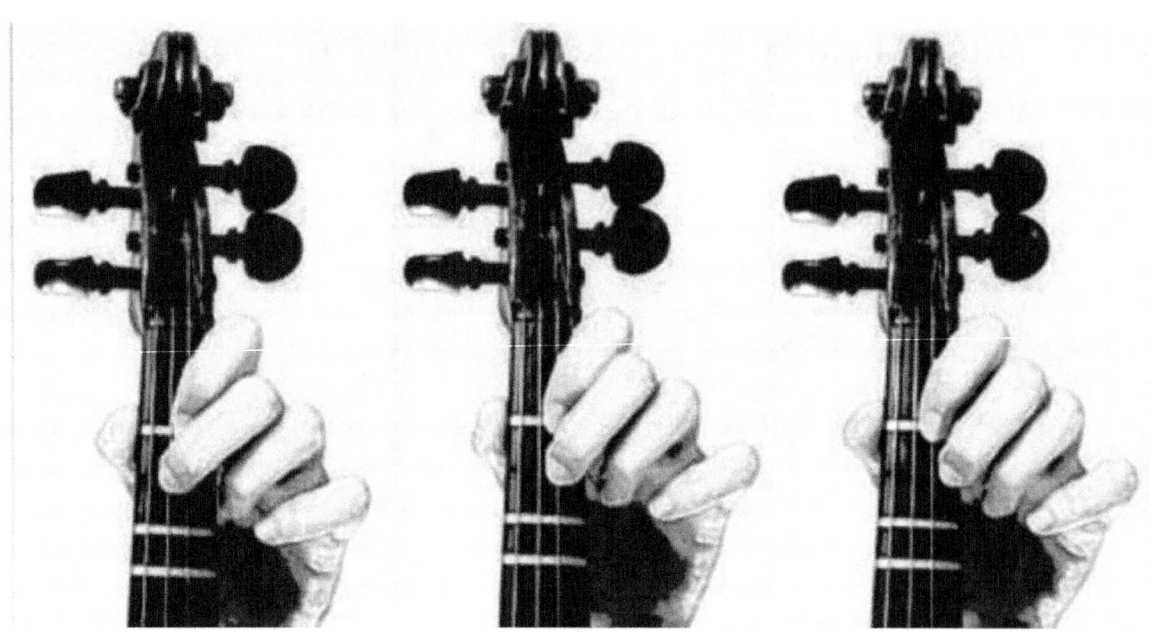

Understanding Your Notes (The Musical ABC)

The eight notes form the musical ABCs: ABCDEFG. This pattern repeats itself to fill all ranges of notes in pitch, and an octave is called an eight-note series. That is why you need to tune your strings to a specific pitch level; for example, in music, G3 is the 3rd G octave. A composer can adjust a note in three ways to add color or different moods to a song: Flat, Natural and Sharp.

Flat, Natural and Sharp symbols

Every note is natural unless otherwise indicated by a flat symbol or a sharp sign, so it is normal to see a note without a symbol which automatically means that the note is performed as natural.

Finger Patterns

Finger patterns show you where each finger on all four strings is flat, natural, and sharp, like a road map that helps streamline your finger movements. There are four patterns to learn with your fingers: High 2, Low 2, Low 1, and High 3. Each finger pattern contains a certain combination of fingers; for instance the High 2 finger pattern allows the violinist to concentrate on all four strings only on the gold tape notes.

Easy way to practice the bow with all four finger patterns:

1.   Place the violin, hand, and fingers under the violin and swing the elbow to the right, so your fingers can reach the G string. Place a straight bow at the frog on the string G.

2.   Set the finger, or prepare by lifting the fingers off the string to play an open string.

3.   Say the name of a note out loud with its accompanying symbol.

4.   Use your full range of motion in both a long, smooth, down bow and repeat the note with a long smooth, upward bow.

5.   Repeat 2–4 steps.

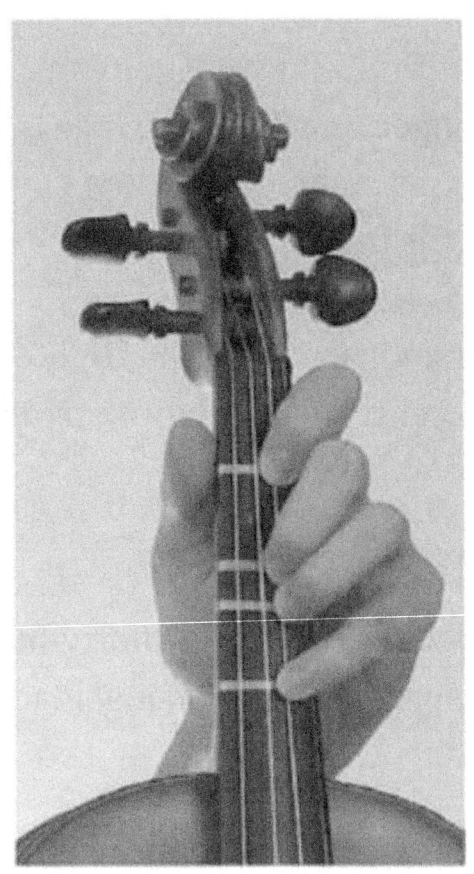

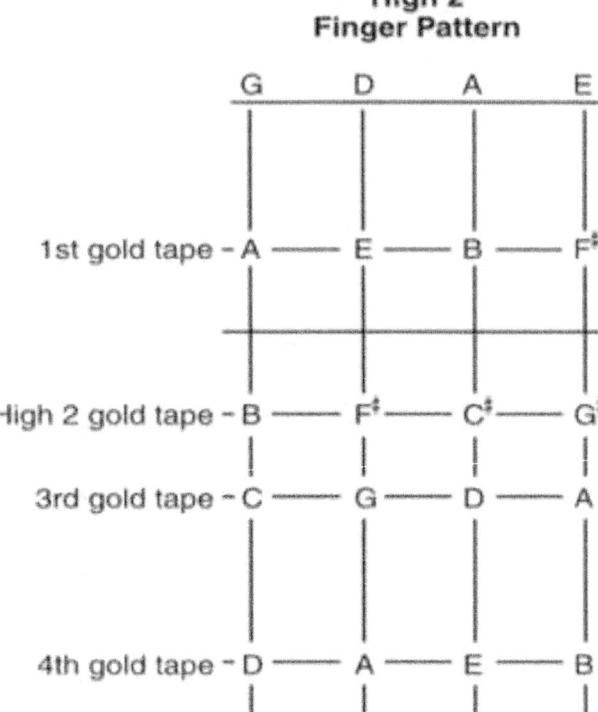

High 2
Finger Pattern

	G	D	A	E
1st gold tape –	A	E	B	F♯
High 2 gold tape –	B	F♯	C♯	G♯
3rd gold tape –	C	G	D	A
4th gold tape –	D	A	E	B

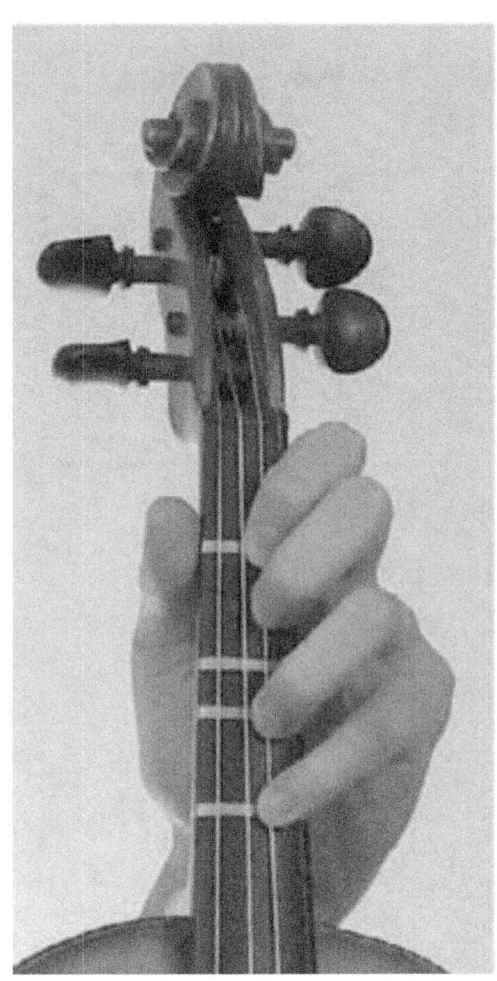

Low 2
Finger Pattern

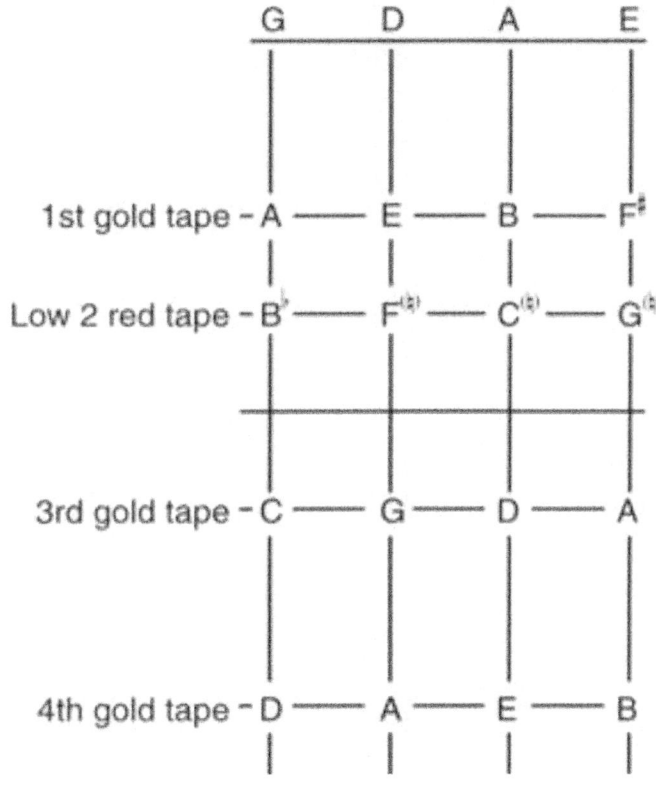

	G	D	A	E
1st gold tape –	A	E	B	F♯
Low 2 red tape –	B♭	F(♮)	C(♮)	G(♮)
3rd gold tape –	C	G	D	A
4th gold tape –	D	A	E	B

45

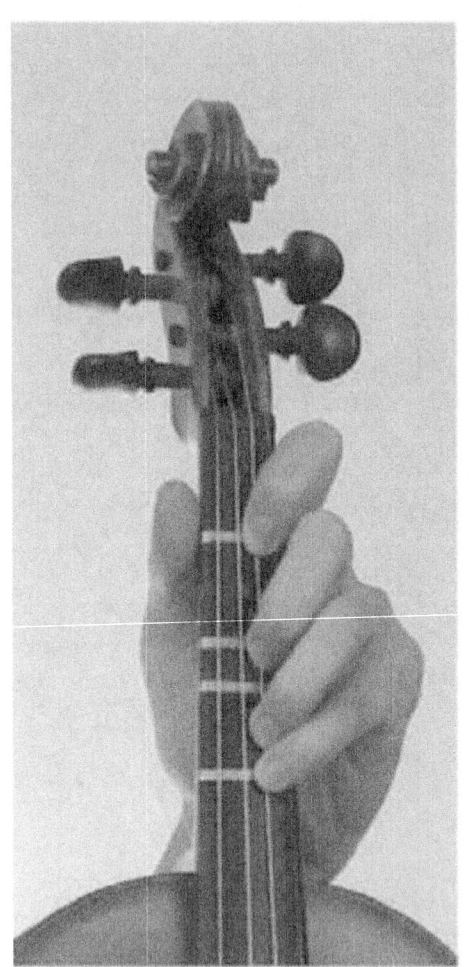

High 3
Finger Pattern

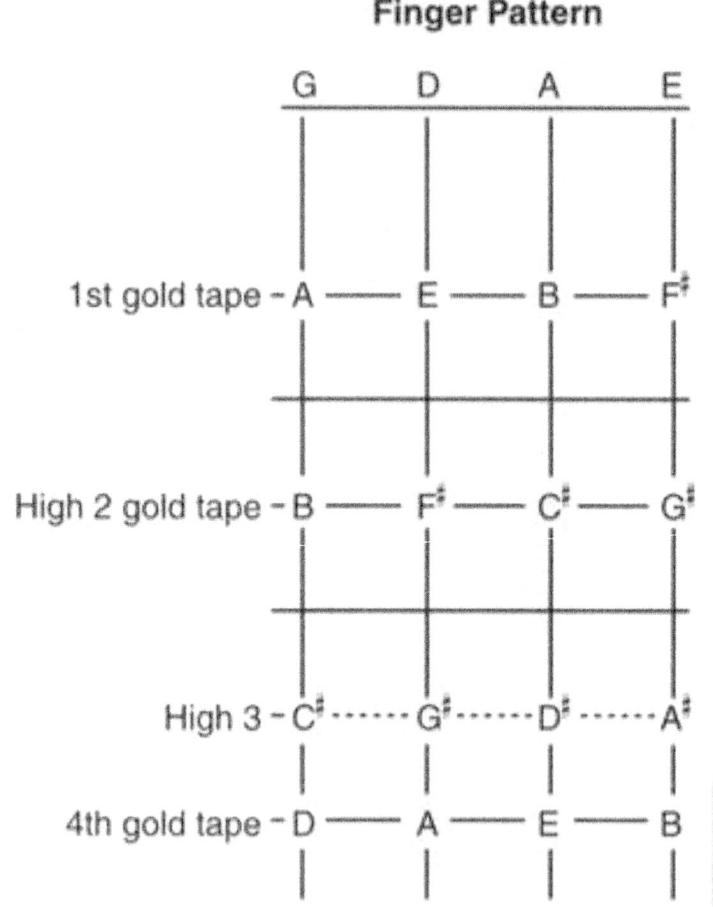

	G	D	A	E
1st gold tape –	A	E	B	F$^\sharp$
High 2 gold tape –	B	F$^\sharp$	C$^\sharp$	G$^\sharp$
High 3 –	C$^\sharp$	G$^\sharp$	D$^\sharp$	A$^\sharp$
4th gold tape –	D	A	E	B

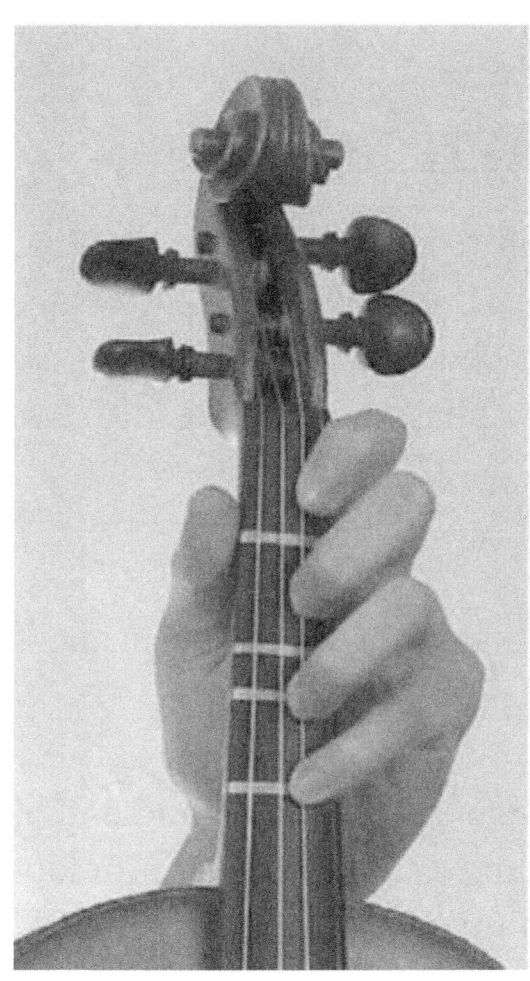

Low 1
Finger Pattern

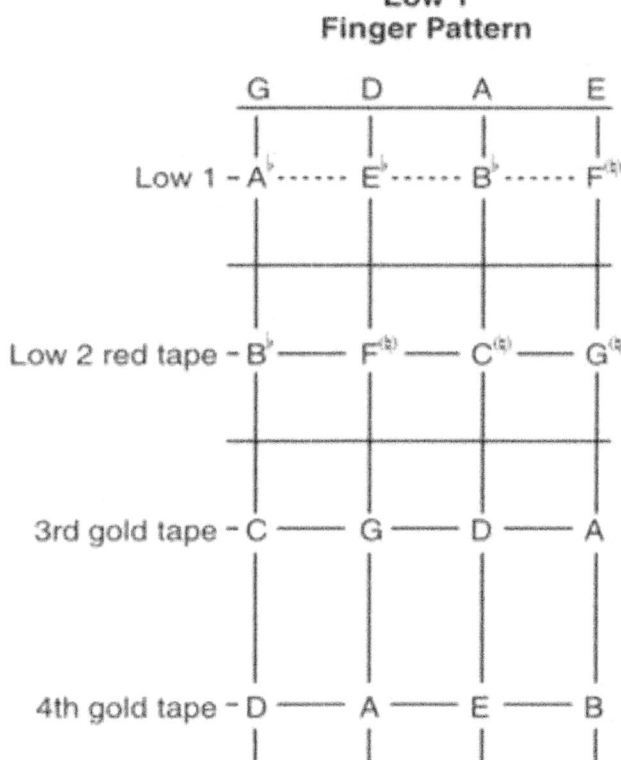

	G	D	A	E
Low 1 –	A♭	E♭	B♭	F$^{(♮)}$
Low 2 red tape –	B♭	F$^{(♮)}$	C$^{(♮)}$	G$^{(♮)}$
3rd gold tape –	C	G	D	A
4th gold tape –	D	A	E	B

CHAPTER FIVE

UNDERSTANDING FINGER-PATTERN SLURS

A little exercise called Finger-Pattern Slurs is the final step to achieving full mobility on the violin. This blends discrete patterns of your fingers on a single string with a new bowing technique called the slur. A slur is when you play a single bow stroke with two or more notes.

Easy way to slur notes together:

1. Place the violin, wrist, and fingers in playing position, and start with your bow at the frog on the A string.

2. Slur two notes: use half of the bow for an open A and half of the bow for 1st finger B by pulling a smooth and continuous bow (almost). Just put your 1st finger on the string when you get to the middle of the bow without stopping the bow.

3. Try the new technique of bowing up bow (almost) by starting with the first finger B and lifting it to open A.

Two-note slur, down bow

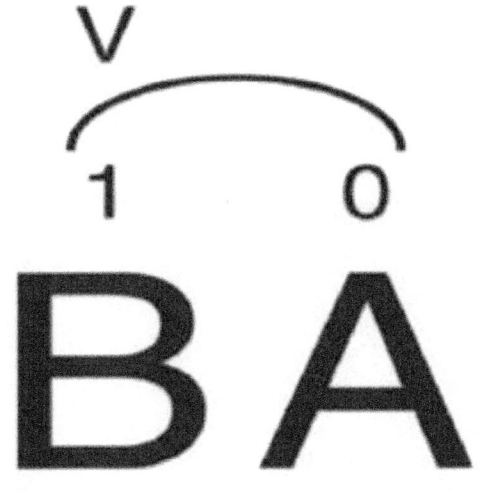

Two-note slur, up bow

4. Slur three notes: divide the bow into thirds and play open A, 1st finger B, and high 2 C, all in the same bow down. On the up bow, reverse the fingerings, begin with the High 2, 1st finger and then open A.

5. Slur four notes: split your bow into fourths playing open A, first finger B, high 2 C), and third finger D, all slurred down bow. Turn the finger to bow, start with the 3rd finger, High 2, 1st finger, then open A..

6. Slur five notes: Slur the open A through the 4th finger with a gentle bow and reverse the upward fingering.

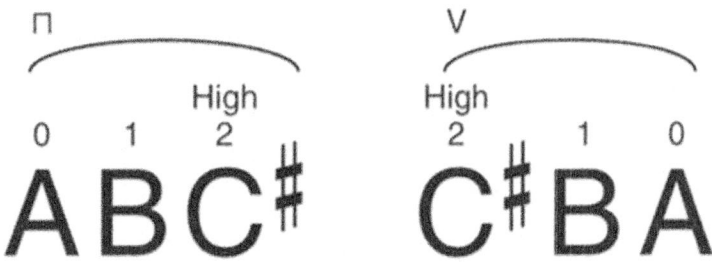

Three-note slur, down and up bow

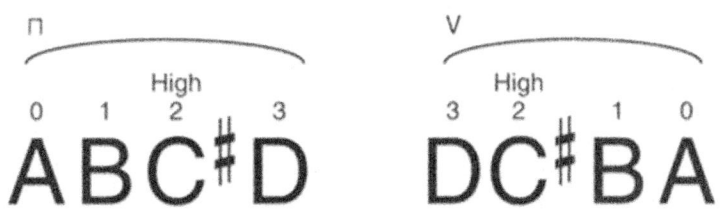

Four-note slur, down and up bow

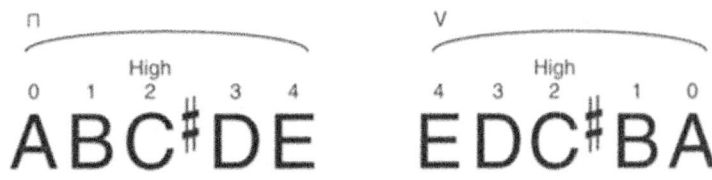

Five-note slur, down and up bow

CHAPTER SIX

READING MUSICAL NOTES

In music, notes are divided into line notes and space notes. The placement of the note head on the staff shows the musician its name and which string it relates to on the violin.

The Line Notes

Line notes sit on the five lines of a staff. You can say a note is a line note by noting that the staff line cuts right through the middle of the head of the note. There's an easy saying to help you memorize the line notes order from the bottom to the top of the staff: Every Good Boy Does Fine.

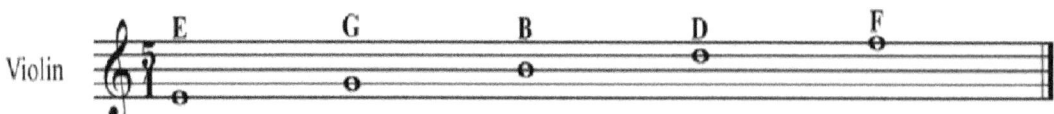

Space Notes

Space notes sit on the four spaces of a staff. You can tell a note is a space note by observing that the lines of the staff are above and below the note head. There is an easy word that can help you memorize the order of the space notes from the bottom to the top of the staff: FACE.

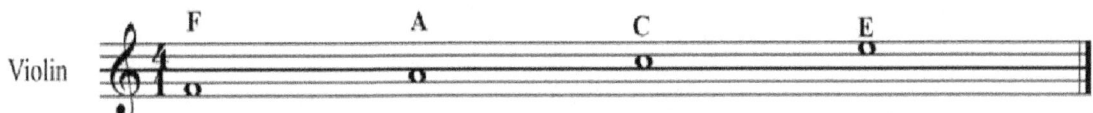

Violin Strings Notes

The staff is assigned four notes to each of the four violin strings, with a repeating note 4th finger. Now you can compare side by side how the patterns of the fingers correlate with the notes on the staff.

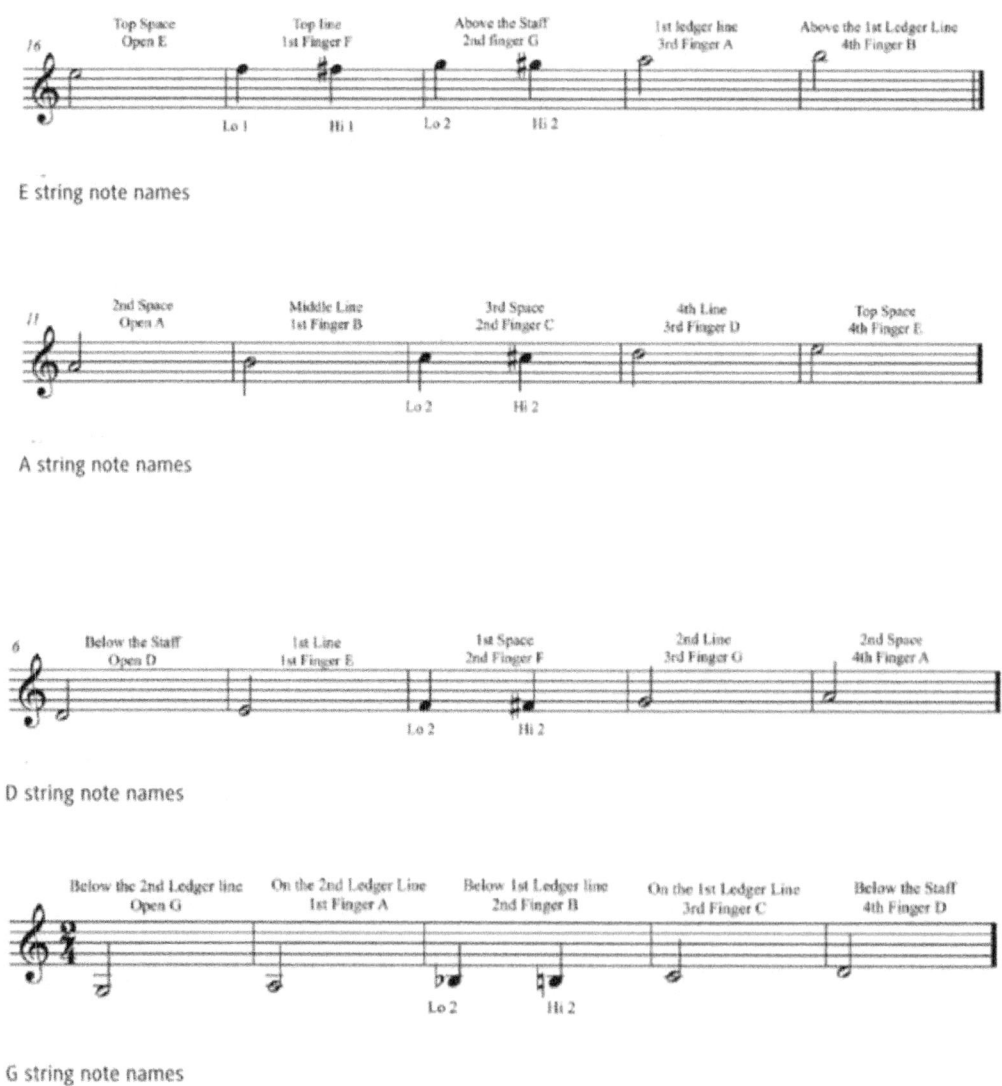

E string note names

A string note names

D string note names

G string note names

OCTAVES

An octave is an eight note series. You can have the same note repeated an octave higher in music, for instance note G is played as Open G, 3rd finger G on string D, and Low 2 G on string E. It's a good idea to learn where each octave is on the violin, so that you can better understand which G is correlated to which G is on the violin.

violin octaves

Having understood how to position, hold the violin and the bow, how to identify and read the different types of musical notes, we will now progress to the last chapter of the book that contains practice exercises.

Common Questions and Answers

Learning to play the violin can be very mind boggling. Individuals regularly have a great deal of inquiries concerning the procedure. What's the most ideal approach to learn? To what extent does it take to get great? When will you begin to have the option to play the melodies you need to play? Continue perusing to become familiar with the responses to a portion of these normal inquiries.

Q: How Long Does it Take to Learn to Play Violin?

An: It truly relies upon you. What amount do you practice? Where are you learning?

A few people can get incredibly, great in under 3 months. Others take 3 years to get great. To put it plainly, there is nobody equation that chooses how rapidly somebody gets the hang of the violin.

Q: Should I Hire a Private Tutor?

A: sooner or later, truly, completely. However, not at the outset.

A great many people don't understand that learning from a mentor as a novice is moderate and over the top expensive. You'll see that your learning velocity will be radically chopped down on the grounds that you'll frequently need to sit tight for exercises before you can improve.

You'll spend numerous exercises to start with learning the nuts and bolts like tuning or stance or music hypothesis. As a general rule, this can be learned a lot quicker without anyone else at home.

Q: What is the Best Way to Learn to Play Violin?

A: The most ideal approach to figure out how to play the violin is with a mix of online recordings and coaching when you need it.

You can really gain totally from online recordings. Numerous individuals do. It's a lot quicker and more affordable than learning from a guide face to face.

Notwithstanding, on the off chance that you at any point do go over a barrier that you truly need assistance with, enlisting a private coach can help you through that barricade. Other than that however, learning alone is commonly quicker.

Q: How Long Will it Take Before I Can Play the Songs I Want?

An: It depends how much time and exertion you put into it. For straightforward tunes, you can be playing them in as meager as 2-3 months. For complex tunes, you can be playing them in as meager as a half year, maybe significantly quicker on the off chance that you truly put in the work.

On the other hand, it could take months or years, contingent upon the amount you practice and how you learn.

CHAPTER SEVEN

PRACTICE EXERCISES

The practice exercises in this chapter are grouped in two. The first part is practice exercises of musical notes and the second part is practice exercises for songs. After gaining mastery of the musical notes, you will find it easier to play the songs.

1st–4th fingers on each string

Step-wise Notes:

Skips on Spaces: **Skips on Lines:**

Intervals

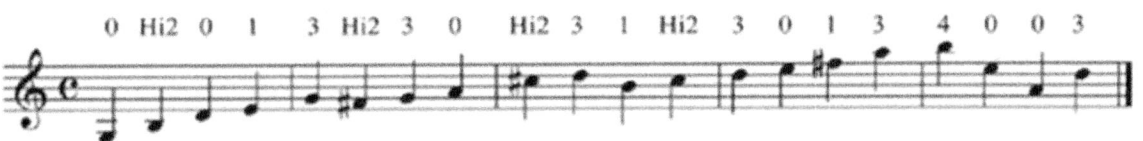

Mixtures

Practice Exercise 1 (Musical Notes)

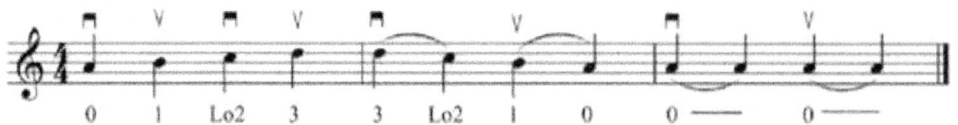

Legato notes

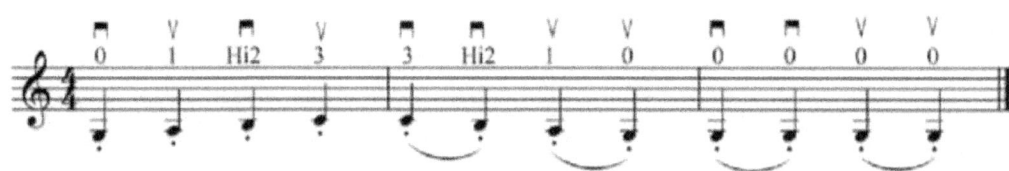

Staccato notes

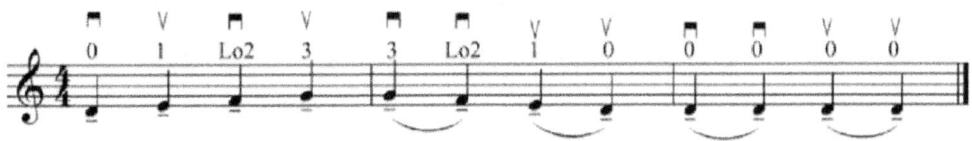

Detache notes

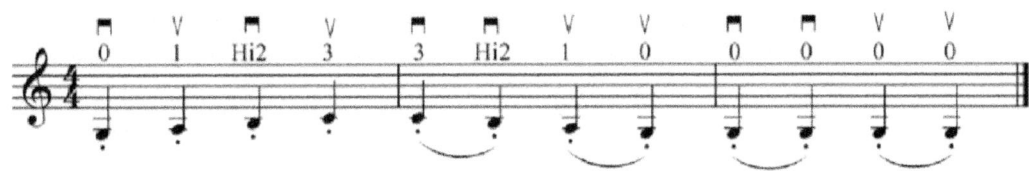

Staccato notes

Spiccato notes

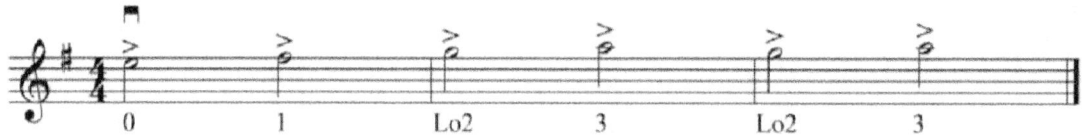

Accent notes

martale notes

Martale resets

Ricochet notes

Tremolo notes

Decrescendo

Practice Exercise 2 (Songs)

Lightly Row

Violin

Go Tell Aunt Rhody

Ode to Joy

Folk Song

Yellow Rose of Texas

68

Violin

On Top of Old Smoky

J. Offenbach

Can-Can

70

Books by the same author:

Search: "Louis Harris"

on Amazon

Kind reader,

Thank you very much, I hope you enjoyed the book.

Can I ask you a big favor?

I would be grateful if you would please take a few minutes to leave me a gold star on Amazon.

Thank you again for your support.

Louis Harris

Printed in Dunstable, United Kingdom

67628175R00045